SEMIOTEXT(E) INTERVENTION SERIES

Copyright © Paul B. Preciado, 2020

Translation copyright © Frank Wynne, 2021

First published in 2020 as *Je suis un monstre qui vous parle* by Éditions Grasset, Paris.

This edition first published by Semiotext(e) in 2021, by arrangement with Casanovas & Lynch Agency, Barcelona.

Published by Semiotext(e)
PO BOX 629, South Pasadena, CA 91031
www.semiotexte.com

Design: Hedi El Kholti

ISBN: 978-1-63590-151-1
Distributed by the MIT Press, Cambridge, Mass., and London, England
Printed in the United States of America

10 9 8 7 6 5 4 3 2

Paul B. Preciado

Can the Monster Speak?

Report to an Academy of Psychoanalysts

Translated by Frank Wynne

semiotext(e)
intervention
series □ 32

I would like to thank Virginie Despentes for her reading of this text and for her unconditional support.

For Judith Butler

SPEECH GIVEN BY A TRANS MAN
BY A NON-BINARY BODY
BEFORE THE ÉCOLE DE LA CAUSE FREUDIENNE
IN FRANCE

On November 17, 2019, I was invited to the Palais des congrès in Paris to give a speech to 3,500 psychoanalysts who had gathered as part of the 49th Study Day of the École de la Cause Freudienne on the theme "Women in psycho-analysis." The speech triggered an earthquake. When I asked whether there was a psychoanalyst in the auditorium who was queer, trans or non-binary, there was silence, broken only by giggles. When I asked that psychoanalytic institutions face up to their responsibilities in response to contem-porary discursive changes in the epistemology of sexual and gender identity, half the audience laughed and the other half shouted or demanded that I leave the premises. One woman said, loudly enough that I could hear her from the rostrum: "We shouldn't allow him to speak, he's Hitler." Half of the auditorium applauded and cheered. The organizers reminded me that my allocated time had run out, I tried to speed up, skipped several paragraphs, I managed to read only a quarter of my prepared speech.

In the days that followed, psychoanalytic organizations tear each other apart. The École de la Cause Freudienne is split, the pro- and anti-positions become more sharply defined. The speech, which has been chaotically filmed by dozens of mobile phones, is posted on the internet, fragments of the text are transcribed without anyone requesting my original text, then these are translated into Spanish, Italian and English and published online with little care for the accuracy of the words or the quality of the translations. As a result, approximate versions of the speech now circulate in Argentina, Colombia, Germany, Spain and France. In order to broaden the debate, I would now like to publish the complete text as I would have wished to share it with the gathering of psychoanalysts.

"What am I doing here? I have come to terrorize you! I am a monster, you say? No! I am the people! I am an exception? No! I am the rule; you are the exception!
You are the chimera; I am the reality!"
—Victor Hugo, *The Man Who Laughs* (1869), quoted by artist Lorenza Böttner in her thesis "Handicapped?" (1982).

Esteemed ladies and gentlemen of the École de la Cause Freudienne, and I do not know whether it is worth also extending a greeting to all those who are neither ladies nor gentlemen, because I doubt that there is anyone among you who has publicly and legally repudiated sexual difference and been accepted as a fully-fledged psychoanalyst, having successfully completed the process you refer to as "The Pass," which permits you to practice as an analyst. In this, I am referring to a trans or non-binary psychoanalyst who is accepted by you as an expert. If such a person exists, allow me here and now to offer this dear mutant my warmest greetings.

I have the honor of appearing before the Academy to offer a report on my life as a trans man. I do not know whether I will be able to offer data that you, ladies and gentlemen, academics and psychoanalysts, that you do not already know at first hand, given that you, like me, live within a regime of sex, gender and sexual difference. As a result, almost everything that I can say, you can observe for yourselves on one side or the other of the gender boundary. Although you doubtless consider yourselves to be natural men and women, and such an assumption may have prevented you from observing, from a safe distance, the political framework of which you are part. You will forgive me if, in the course of the story I am about to tell,

I do not take for granted the existence of natural masculinity or femininity. Rest assured, you do not have to abandon your beliefs—and they are beliefs—in order to hear me out. Consider my argument, then go back to your "naturalized" life, if you can.

To introduce myself, since you are a group of 3,500 psychoanalysts and I feel a little alone on this side of the stage, to take a running jump and hoist myself onto the shoulders of the master of metamorphosis, the greatest analyst of the excesses that hide behind the façade of scientific reason and of the madness commonly referred to as mental health: Franz Kafka.

In 1917, Franz Kafka wrote *Ein Bericht für eine Akademie—A Report to an Academy*. The narrator of the text is an ape who, having learned human language, is appearing before an academy of the greatest scientific authorities to report to them on what human evolution has meant to him. The ape, who claims to be called Red Peter, explains how he was captured during a hunting expedition organized by the firm of Hagenbeck, transported to Europe aboard a steamship, is trained to perform in music halls, and how he later sprang into the community of human beings. Red Peter explains that in order to master human language and be accepted in the European society of his time, he had to forget his life as an ape. And how, in order to endure this oblivion and the violence of human society, he became an alcoholic. But the most interesting thing in Red Peter's monologue is that Kafka does not present this process of humanization as a story of emancipation or of liberation from animality, but rather as a critique of colonial European humanism and its anthropological taxonomies. Once captured, the ape says he had no choice: if he did not wish to die locked up in a cage, he had to accept the "cage" of human subjectivity.

Just as the ape Red Peter addressed himself to scientists, so today I address myself to you, the academicians of psychoanalysis, from my "cage" as a trans man. I, a body branded by medical and juridical discourse as "transsexual," characterized in most of your psychoanalytic diagnoses as the subject of an "impossible metamorphosis," find myself, according to most of your theories, beyond neurosis, on the cusp of—or perhaps even within the bounds of—psychosis, being incapable, according to you, of correctly resolving an Oedipus complex or having succumbed to penis envy. And so, it is from the position assigned to me by you as a mentally ill person that I address you, an ape-human in a new era. I am the monster who speaks to you. The monster you have created with your discourse and your clinical practices. I am the monster who gets up from the analyst's couch and dares to speak, not as a patient, but as a citizen, as your monstrous equal.

As a trans body, as a non-binary body, whose right to speak as an expert about my condition, or to produce a discourse or any form of knowledge about myself is not recognized by the medicinal profession, the law, psychoanalysis or psychiatry, I have done as Red Peter did, I have learned the language of Freud and Lacan, the language of the colonial patriarchy, your language, and I am here to address you.

You will perhaps be surprised that, in doing so, I invoke a Kafkaesque tale, but, to me this symposium feels closer to the era of the author of *The Metamorphosis* than to our own. You organize a conference to discuss "women in psychoanalysis" in 2019, as though this were still 1917, as though these exotic animals you casually and condescendingly refer to as "women" have not yet acquired full recognition as political subjects, as though they were an appendix or a footnote, a strange, exotic creature you feel you need to reflect on from time to time in the context of a symposium or a round-table discussion. It might have been better to organize an event on the subject of "white heterosexual middle-class men in psychoanalysis," since most psychoanalytic texts and practices concern themselves with the discursive and political power of this particular beast. A necropolitical[1] animal that you have a tendency to confuse with "universal human" and which remains, at least until the present, the subject of the central statement in the discourses of the psycho-analytical institutions of colonial modernism.

Moreover, I have little to say about "women in psychoanalysis" except that, like Red Peter, I am a renegade. I was, once, a "woman in psychoanalysis." I was assigned female at birth and, like the mutant ape, I extricated myself from that confined "cage," in order to enter another cage, granted, but at least this time through my own initiative.

I speak to you today from this elective, refashioned cage of the "trans man," of the "non-binary body." Some will say that this, too, is a political cage: whatever the case, this cage is better than that of "men and women" in that it acknowledges its status as a cage.

It has been more than six years since I renounced the legal and political status of woman.

---

1. Coined by the Cameroonian post-colonial theorist and historian Achille Mbembe, based on Foucault's concept of "thanatopolitics," the term designates a form of sovereignty that resides in the power to decide who may live and who must die. Necropolitics is the government of peoples through the politics of violence and death.

The period may seem brief when considered in the context of the deadening comfort of normative identity, but infinitely long when everything that has been learned since childhood must be unlearned. When new administrative and political boundaries, invisible yet effective, rise up before you and everyday life becomes an obstacle course. In the life of a trans adult, consequently, six years take on the same importance they have for a newborn in the first months of life, as colors appear before their eyes, as forms take on mass, as hands grip for the first time, as the throat, until now capable only of guttural cries, and the lips, until now used only to suckle, articulate their first word. I bring up the pleasure of childhood learning because a similar pleasure exists in the appropriation of a new voice and a new name, in the exploration of the world beyond the cage of masculinity and femininity that is part of the process of transitioning. Though brief in chronological terms, this period becomes very long when you travel the world, when you find yourself in the media spotlight as the "trending topic" trans; and when, in reality, you are alone when you are required to appear before a psychiatrist, a border guard, a doctor or a judge.

In response to your request to know more about my "transition"—a request I am happy to fulfill, albeit with certain reservations—in these paragraphs

I will set out the path by which an individual who lived as a woman until the age of thirty-eight, having begun by defining themself as a person of non-binary gender, later integrated into the world of men without ever being completely settled in that gender—since, to be acknowledged as a real man, I would have to hold my tongue and dissolve into the naturalized magma of masculinity, never revealing my dissident history or my political past. It should be said that I could not recount the banalities that follow were I not completely sure of myself, were my status as a trans man not already indisputably affirmed in the vast digital media circus throughout the civilized world. Since 16 November 2016, I have held a passport in which the name and gender are masculine, so there are no longer any administrative obstacles to my freedom of movement, or my opportunities to speak out.

I was assigned female at birth in a little Catholic town in a Spain still ruled by Franco. The die was cast. Girls were now allowed to do most of the things that boys did. What was expected of me was the execution of the silent, conscientious and reproductive work appropriate to my assigned gender and sexuality. I was expected to grow up to be a dutiful heterosexual girlfriend, a good wife, a good mother, a shy, retiring woman. I grew up listening to whispered stories of young girls being raped, of young women who went to London to have abortions, of lifelong spinster friends who lived together without ever asserting their sexuality in public—"the dykes," as my father contemptuously referred to them. I was trapped. Had I been nailed to the floor, it would not have reduced my scope for action. Why were things as they were? What was it in my child's body that predetermined my whole life? You could scratch yourself until you bled and not find an answer. You could split your head open on the steel bars of gender and not discover the reason.

I also found it impossible to explain the paradox that demanded that women, subjugated, raped, murdered, should not only love, but devote their lives to heterosexual men, their oppressors. I could see no way out, and yet I had to find one: so crushed was I between the walls of masculinity and femininity that I felt I would inevitably die. I was a quiet child, I stayed in my bedroom, I made no noise, from which my parents concluded that, as a body, I would be particularly docile and receptive to a good upbringing. But I resisted domestication, I survived the systematic process intended to extinguish my life force, which governed my childhood and adolescence.

I do not owe this survival instinct to psychoanalysis or psychology, quite the reverse, I owe it to books, to feminist, punk, anti-racist and lesbian books. My temperament was not much suited to socialization, so, for me, books were authentic guides through the desert of fanaticism and sexual difference. Books that—like the works of Giordano Bruno or Galileo that put an end to geocentrism—had been written to put an end to the psychoanalytical conviction that to challenge the binary was tantamount to entering the domain of psychosis. I remember the first time, in a second-hand bookshop in Madrid, when I came across a Spanish translation of Monique Wittig's novel *The Lesbian Body*, in a 1977 edition published by Pre-Textos. I remember the pink cover and the prematurely yellowed pages. As if the title alone were not enough, a paragraph from the book was printed on the back cover: "the lesbian body the juice the spittle the saliva the snot the sweat the tears the wax the urine the feces the excrements the blood the lymph the jelly the water…" While buying it, I did my best to hide the cover from the shop assistant, unable to cope with the shame that, in 1987, came with the desire to buy a book called *The Lesbian Body*. And I remember the bookseller's expression of contempt, but also of relief at the thought that he would finally be rid of this book, as though it were a leaky vessel oozing nauseating slime, sullying his shelves. It cost me 280 pesetas. Its true value, to me, is incalculable. In order to discover the other books that would lead me to where I am today, I had to travel, I had to learn other languages: this was how I discovered Magnus Hirschfeld's *Sappho and Socrates*, Virginia Woolf's *Orlando*, Annemarie Schwarzenbach's *Eine Frau zu sehen* [To See a Woman], the "Rapport contre la normalité" ["Report against Normality"] published by the Front d'Action Révolutionnaire Gay, Guy Hocquenghem's *Homosexual Desire*, Joanna Russ's *The Female Man*, Loren Cameron's *Body Alchemy*, Guillaume Dustan's *In My Room*, the diaries of Lou Sullivan, the novels of Kathy Acker, the feminist rereading of the history of science by Londa Schiebinger, Donna Haraway and Anne Fausto-Sterling, the theoretical texts of Gayle Rubin, Susan Sontag, Judith Butler, Teresa de Lauretis, Eve K. Sedgwick, Jack Halberstam, Susan Striker, Sandy Stone and Karen Barad. Thanks to all these readings I learned to see beauty beyond gender. I grabbed these books and, like a fugitive, I ran as though my heels were on fire, and even today I am still running to escape the serfdom of the binary system of sexual difference. It is thanks to these heretical books that I survived and—more importantly—that I succeeded in imagining a way out.

So, since in the heteropatriarchal binary circus women are offered the role of belle or victim, and since I was not and did not feel myself capable of being one or the other, I decided to stop being a woman. Why couldn't abandoning femininity not become a fundamental tactic of feminism? This amazing association of ideas, lucid and magnificent, must have hatched somewhere in my womb, since women's creativity is said to reside solely in the uterus. And so it must have been in my rebellious, non-reproductive uterus that all the other strategies were conceived: the rage that made me mistrust the norm, the taste for insubordination... Just as children endlessly repeat gestures that give them pleasure and allow them to learn, so I repeated gestures that violated the norm so I could find a way out.

And yet I had no desire to become a man like other men. Their violence and their political arrogance held no attraction for me. I had not the least desire to become what the children of the white middle classes called being normal or healthy. I simply wanted a way out: I didn't care what it was. So I could move forward, so I could escape this mockery of sexual difference, so I would not be arrested, hands in the air, and forced back to the boundaries of this taxonomy. This is how I came to start injecting myself with testosterone, surrounded by a group of friends who were also seeking an exit. This is how this thing that you call "the female condition" burst out from me at breakneck speed, tumbling head over heels, taking me further than I could ever have imagined. Let me repeat myself: I was looking for a door, an exit, a way out.

I fear that people may not quite understand what I mean by the phrase "way out." I use the word in its most common and concrete sense. I carefully avoid using the word freedom, I prefer to speak about finding a way out of the regime of sexual difference, which does not mean instantly becoming free. Personally, I did not experience freedom as a child in Franco's Spain, nor later when I was a lesbian in New York, nor do I experience it now that I am, as they say, a trans man.

Neither then nor now did I ask to be "given" freedom. The powerful constantly promise freedom, but how could they give subalterns something that they themselves do not know? A paradox: they who bind are as imprisoned as they whose movements are hobbled by the knotted ropes. This is no less true of you, esteemed psychoanalysts, the great experts of the unbinding and especially the rebinding of the unconscious, the great promoters of promises or of health and freedom. No one can give what they do not have and what they have never known. Indeed, we enthusiastically allow ourselves to be deceived when it comes to "men" and "women" in the hoary clichés of sexual "liberation," since liberty is among the values most often promoted; moreover, the sham to which it corresponds is the most facile in the domain of gender and sexuality. These days, liberal feminism is fashionable, and so an increasing number of men and women do not hesitate to call themselves feminists, though not without stressing the stipulation, essential to them, that women must remain women and men must remain men. But what are they talking about when they talk about nature? Similarly, when a "man" takes responsibility for a tiny share of the housework, people talk about it and herald it as progress in the equality of the sexes and women's liberation. These acts of liberation make me laugh so hard that my chest quivers like a drumskin danced on by a centipede. Liberation, whether gender or sexual, cannot under any circumstances be a more equitable redistribution of violence, nor a more pop acceptance of oppression. Liberty is a tunnel that must be dug by hand. Freedom is a way out. Liberty—like the new name by which you now call me, or the vaguely hirsute face you see before you—is something that is carefully fabricated and exercised.

And my way out, among other things, was testosterone. In this process, the hormone is not an end in itself: it is an ally in the task of inventing an elsewhere. So I have gradually abandoned the framework of sexual difference. The artist Del LaGrace Volcano says that to be trans is to be intersex by design. And this is exactly what happened. Gradually, as the testosterone worked on my features, my body and my muscles, it became difficult to keep my official identity as female. So began the problems of crossing borders. We live within the political net of sexual difference, and here I am not referring just to administrative issues, but to a whole series of micro-powers that act on our bodies and model our behaviors. When I realized that leaving the regime of sexual difference meant leaving the human sphere and entering into a subaltern space of violence and control, I—like Galileo, when he recanted his heliocentric hypotheses—did everything necessary to carry on living as well as I could and I demanded a place within the binary gender regime.

Assigned female at birth, and living as a supposedly emancipated woman, I began digging a tunnel, I accepted the burden of identifying as transsexual and, consequently, I accepted the fact that my condition, my body, my psyche would, according to the knowledge you profess and defend, be considered pathological. Let me tell you, however, that in this apparent state of constraint I managed to fabricate greater freedom than I had had as a supposedly free woman in the technopatriarchal society of the early twenty-first century, if by freedom we mean the ability to go out, to perceive a horizon, to build a project, to experience if only for a fleeting instant the radical community of all life, all energy, all matter beyond the taxonomic hierarchies invented by human history. If the regime of sexual difference can be conceived as a semio-technical and cognitive framework that limits our perception, or ways of feeling and loving, the journey of gender transitioning, however tortuous and erratic it may appear, made it possible for me to experience life beyond these limits.

And as paradoxical as it might seem, the tunnel towards a way out, in my case, would go via a strict, academic education in the very languages by which my body and my subjectivity had been fettered. In the same way that the professor in *Money Heist* studied the invisible architecture of a bank so he could devise a strategy, not to break in, but to get the loot out, which was more complicated, I studied the cognitive architecture of sexual difference, knowing full well that, in my case, it would be much more difficult to find the loot and get away with it. In the infinite labyrinth of institutions in our society dealing with the construction of the "truths" of gender and sexuality, I found many teachers: I visited numerous universities, I learned the language of philosophers, psychoanalysts and sociologists, of doctors, historians, architects and biologists. Oh, when you need to learn, you learn; when you need to find a way out, you learn relentlessly! You whip yourself into shape, flagellate yourself for the slightest weakness. What progress! What progress in every sphere of knowledge, in the ignorant brain of a simple transsexual prepared to put a shoulder to the wheel! And since intellectual tools making it possible to deconstruct dominant thought began appearing in the academic domain in the 1970s, following post-colonial critique and the gradual emancipation of the feminist, gay and working-class movements, I had access, not only to normative discourses, but also to numerous subaltern forms of knowledge that brought together the experiences of resistance, struggle and political emancipation of those who, historically, had been subjected to extermination, violence and control. I studied Black and lesbian feminist traditions, anti-colonial critiques and post-Marxist movements. This learning process made me happy. Through an unprecedented exertion, given my supposed condition as a person suffering from mental illness and dysphoria, I managed to acquire the education of your average white bourgeois European. When I was awarded my doctorate at Princeton University and I saw a new group of instructors applaud me, I realized that I had to be circumspect. Here it is again, the cage: gilded this time, but just as solid as those I had known before. My predecessor, Red Peter, claimed that he "beat his way through the bushes," and that is precisely what I did, I beat my way through the bushes of academia...

And it was doubtless thanks to my status as a "doctor" that I saw the journey become simpler, although for most trans persons it is a journey that represents a formidable ordeal: the task of getting new identity papers in a binary society. After a number of visits to various psychologists who could award me the "good transsexual" certificate that would allow me to get new identity papers, I quickly understood that there were two paths open to me: the pharmacological and psychiatric route to domesticated transsexuality and, with it, the anonymity of normal masculinity or, on the other hand, and in opposition to this, the spectacle of political writing. I did not hesitate. Normal, naturalized masculinity was nothing other than a new cage. Those who enter will never leave. And I chose. I said to myself: speak publicly. Don't silence yourself. And so, of my body, my mind and my monstrosity, of my desire and my transition, I made a public spectacle: yet again, I had found a way out. This is how I escaped my medical handlers, who looked a lot like you, esteemed academics and psychoanalysts. Let's say I had no other route, always assuming that it was not a case of *choosing* freedom but of *creating* it.

Although I was regularly self-administering testosterone, it was only much later that I was acknowledged as a man in society. Firstly, though I already had a wispy beard and a mustache, the binary creatures of the heteropatriarchal society persisted in calling me "madame," they eyed me contemptuously as they did so, sometimes they would mutter the word "dyke" when my back was turned. Until the day when, after three months spent injecting myself with testosterone, 250 mg every twenty-one days, I opened my mouth and a hoarse, gravelly voice came from my throat. I was more startled than anyone, it was as though my vocal tract were possessed by an alien being. It was not the masculine nature of the voice that terrified me, but the difference between it and the voice by which everyone had recognized me until then. Then I went out into the street and started talking with this voice that was at once mine and someone else's. My first words propelled me into the community of those who think of themselves as men, who welcomed me as never before: "Listen to him talk, he's a man!" To me these words felt like a branding iron, taken from the flames, marking me out as a man, finally accepting me into the masculine community. That first day, my triumph was short-lived, because immediately afterwards, my voice cracked and failed me once again. Little by little, this alien voice became a part of me. It is with this voice, fabricated yet organic, staged yet entirely my own, that I address you today, esteemed ladies and gentlemen of the Academy.

When I first began this process of transition, it took me some time to decipher the codes of dominant masculinity. And, believe it or not, nothing was more difficult than getting used to the stench and the filth of men's toilets. I was tormented by the smell, by the pools of urine splashed over and around lavatories and, despite my best intentions, it took weeks before I managed to overcome this revulsion. Up until the moment when I realized that this filth, this stench, corresponded to a kind of strictly homosocial relationship: men had created a fetid circle to keep women at bay. Inside the circle, in secret, they were free to look at each other, to touch each other, free to wallow in their own bodily fluids, away from any representation of heterosexuality. Whereas women go to the bathroom to recreate their mask of femininity, men go there to forget their heterosexuality for an instant and revel in the pleasure of being alone, away from the strange alter egos that are the women by whom they must be accompanied in society to fulfill a reproductive and heteroconsensual role. Through this experience, and many others that were even weirder that I don't have time to detail here, I began to sense that things were more and more ridiculous, but also more complex and more multifaceted than I could have imagined when I still held the political status of a woman. The masks of the dominant strain of femininity and masculinity, of normative heterosexuality, concealed multiple forms of resistance and deviance.

The first thing I learned as a trans person was how to walk down the street and be seen by others as a man. I learned to look directly ahead and slightly up rather than looking sideways or down. I learned to look other men in the eye, without turning away and without smiling. But the most important thing that I discovered is that, in the patriarchal-colonial system, being a so-called "man" and so-called "white," I could accede for the first time to the privilege of universality. A peaceful and anonymous place where everyone leaves you the fuck alone. I had never felt universal. I had been a woman, I had been a lesbian, I had been a migrant. I had known otherness, not universality. If I did not publicly announce myself as "trans" and accepted being acknowledged as a man, I could shrug off the burden of identity once and for all.

Why is it, my beloved binary friends, that you are convinced that only subalterns possess an identity? Why are you convinced that only Muslims, Jews, queers, lesbians, trans folk, people who live in the *banlieues*, migrants and Blacks have an identity? Do you therefore believe that you—the normal, the hegemonic, the bourgeois white psychoanalysts, the binary, the patriarchal-colonials—have no identity? There is no identity more rigid and sclerotic than your invisible identity. Than your republican universality. Your weightless, anonymous identity is the privilege of sexual, racial and gender norms. Either everyone has an identity. Or there is no identity. We all occupy a distinct place in a complex network of power relations. To be branded with an identity means simply that one does not have the power to designate one's identity as universal. There is no universality in the psychoanalytic tales you recount. The mytho-psychological tales picked up by Freud and raised to the rank of science by Lacan are simply local stories, tales of the patriarchal-colonial European mind, tales used to legitimize the sovereign power of the white father over all other bodies. Psychoanalysis is an ethnocentrism that refuses to recognize its political position. And I do not say this to bow before ethnopsychiatry whose hypotheses are equally patriarchal-colonial and are not different from those of psychoanalysis in terms of the naturalization of sexual difference.

Since normative psychoanalysis and psychology give meaning to the process of subjectification in accordance with the gender-binary heterosexual regime of sexual difference, any non-heterosexual sexuality, any process of gender transition or any identification as gender non-binary triggers a raft of diagnoses. One of the fundamental strategies of psychoanalytical discourse is to uncover symptoms of illness in the prenatal or infantile development of the homosexual, or the transsexual, or gender non-binary person, to investigate the trauma that triggers inversion. Some among you will say that in becoming "trans" I have renounced my true female nature. Others will say that there was within me a pre-existing masculine nature (whether defined in terms of genetics, endocrinology or psychology) that sought to express itself. Still others will say that it was the secret desires of my parents (invariably imaged as a binary heterosexual, preferably white couple) that surfaced in me and made me what I am today. Bullshit. These are no more than grotesque simplifications. I am not at all what you imagine. It is no easier to know who an individual is than to determine the precise location of an electron in a particle accelerator.

Contrary to the claims of colonial, hetero-patriarchal psychiatry and psychoanalysis, there was no desire in my childhood to be a "man" that might legitimize or justify my transition. Had I clung stubbornly to what you call "my origins," had I simply followed the ideas of my childhood, my parents' desires, limited by education, punishment and fear, it would have been impossible for me to achieve what I have achieved. In order to transform, I set myself two laws greater than all the rules the patriarchal-colonial society tried to instill in me. The first law, which I considered self-evident during the whole process of my transition, was to do away with the fear of being abnormal that had been planted in my heart as a child. It is this fear that needs to be identified, quarantined and eliminated from memory. The second law, one that was rather more difficult to observe, was to be wary of all simplification. To cease to assume, as you do, that I know what a man is, what a woman is, what a homosexual or a heterosexual is. To free my thinking from these shackles and experience, try to perceive, to feel, to name, beyond sexual difference.

Today, it is clear to me: had I not been indifferent to the ordered, purportedly happy world of the norm, had I not been thrown out by my own family, had I not preferred my monstrosity to your heteronormativity, had I not chosen my sexual deviance over your sexual health, I would never have been able to escape...or, to be more precise, would never have been able to decolonize, disidentify, debinarify myself. In leaving the cage of sexual difference, I experienced ostracization and social rejection, but none of that was as disastrous, as painful, as the destruction of my life force, which would have been required of me in accepting the norm. Everything I have become I probably owe to the indifference to mental health I developed during my teenage years, buoyed up by books, in that Spanish town where it seemed that my future had been written by God Himself, and later translated into various languages by doctors and psychoanalysts.

My life outside the regime of sexual difference is more glorious than anything you could have promised me as a reward for subscribing to the norm. If I accepted the new yoke of a male name in the middle of this tunnel towards the way out, it was the better to demonstrate the sophistry that underlies all gender identifications. This yoke has also brought with it certain advantages which I accept from time to time like a glass of water in a political desert. Those unaware that I am trans treat me with the prerogatives and the deference accorded to white men in patriarchal-colonial society. Doubtless, I could profit from these fatuous favors, but to do so I would have had (an impossible task!) to lose my memory.

Not only have the memories of the life I spent as a woman not been expunged, but they remain vivid in my mind such that, contrary to what medicine and psychiatry believe and promulgate, I have not completely ceased to be Beatriz to become solely Paul. My living body, I will not say my unconscious or my consciousness, but my living body, which encompasses all its constant mutation and its multiple evolutions, is like a Greek city in which, at varying levels of energy, contemporary trans buildings, postmodern lesbian architecture and beautiful Art Deco houses coexist with ancient rustic buildings beneath whose foundations lie classical ruins both animal and vegetal, mineral and chemical substrates that tend to be invisible. The traces of past life left in my memory have become more and more complex and interconnected, creating a collection of living forces, such that it is impossible to say that only six years ago I was *simply* a woman and today I have become *simply* a man. I prefer my new condition as monster to that of man or woman, because his condition is like a foot stepping forward into the void, indicating the path to another world. Here, I am not speaking of the living body as an anatomical object, but as what I call "somatheque," a living political archive. In the same way that Freud spoke of a psychic apparatus greater than consciousness, so today it is necessary to postulate a new notion of the somatic apparatus to take into account the historic and externalized modalities of the body, those that exist and are mediated through digital, pharmacological, biochemical and prosthetic technologies. The somatheque is mutating.

The monster is one who lives in transition. One whose face, body and behaviors cannot yet be considered true in a predetermined regime of knowledge and power.

To transition is to come to a machinic arrangement with the hormone of some other living code—the code may be a language, a music, a gesture, a plant, an animal or another living creature. To transition is to establish a transversal communication with the hormone which erases or, better still, eclipses what you call the female phenotype and allows for the awakening of another genealogy. This awakening is revolution. It is a molecular uprising. An assault on the power of the hetero-patriarchal ego, of identity and of name. The process is a decolonization of the body.

It is the potential revolution inherent in any process of transition that terrifies normative psychology and psychoanalysis which do everything they can to neutralize its power. In the dominant medical and psychological discourse, the trans body is a colony.

The trans body is to heteronormativity what Lesbos is to Europe: a border whose form and extent can be perpetuated only through violence. Cut here, paste there, remove these organs, replace them with others.

The trans body is a colony. Every day, on some street in Tijuana or Los Angeles, Saint Petersburg or Goa, Athens or Seville, a trans body is killed with the same impunity that a new occupied settlement is built on one bank or the other of the River

Jordan. Medicine and clinical psychology are waging a war to impose and standardize the organs of the trans body.

The migrant has lost the nation state. The refugee has lost their house. The trans person loses their body. They all cross that border. The border is part of them and cuts through them. Usurps and overthrows them.

The trans body is to the epistemology of sexual difference what the American continents were to the Spanish empire: a place of such richness and culture that it beggared the imperial imagination. A place of mining and extermination of life. Our trans organs are to the heteropatriarchal system what the Potosí silver mines were to the patriarchal-colonial unconscious. The silver is extracted from the earth and the miner is buried in a shaft. Our organs are Amazonian rubber and the gold of the Sierras. Our organs are the oil that the normative sexual machine requires in order to function. Everywhere, the trans body is hated, and, at the same time, fantasized, desired and consumed.

The trans body is a life force, it is the inexhaustible Amazon flowing through the rainforests, impervious to dams and to mining.

The trans body is to normative anatomy what Africa once was to Europe: a territory to be carved up and handed over to the highest bidder. The breasts and the skin to cosmetic surgery, the vagina to state surgery, the penis to psychiatry or to Lacanian anamorphosis. What Western scientific and technical discourse considers to be the emblematic sexual organs of masculinity and femininity, the penis and the vagina, are no more real than Rwanda or Nigeria, than Spain or Italy. There is a difference between the lush green hill on one bank of a river and the windswept desert that stretches away on the other bank. There is the erotic landscape of the body. There are no sexual organs, only colonial enclaves of power.

The trans body is a colony of disciplinary institutions, of psychoanalysis, of the media, of the pharmaceutical industry, of the market.

The trans body is Africa; its organs, though living, speak in languages unknown to the colonizer, they have dreams that you, psychoanalysts, are unaware of.

When you have cut down all the trees and mined all the mountains, when you have analyzed all your dreams, there will be nothing left for you to break. The Earth then will be a rubbish dump, a vast trans body dismembered and devoured. The bodies of the colonists and your bodies, esteemed psychoanalysts, will be buried with the trans organs you have taken from us. But the organs that we do not have can never be buried. Our utopian organs will live on eternally. They will be the warriors storming the borders.

In the midst of this patriarchal-colonial war, gender transition is an antigenealogy. It entails activating those genes whose expression had been thwarted by the presence of estrogens, by connecting them via testosterone and triggering a parallel evolution of my own life, by giving free expression to the phenotype that would otherwise have remained silent. To be trans, one must accept the triumphant irruption of another future in oneself, in every cell of one's body. To transition comes down to understanding that the cultural codes of masculinity and femininity are anecdotal compared to the infinite variety of modalities of existence.

Mimetism is a poor tool when thinking about gender transition since it still relies on binary logic. To be this or that, to be one thing and imitate something else. Either you are a man, or you are a woman. A trans person is not imitating anything, just as a crocodile is not imitating a floating tree trunk, or a chameleon the colors of the world.

To be trans is to cease to be a crocodile and connect with one's vegetal future, to understand that the rainbow can become a skin.

When accepted as a techno-shamanistic process triggered by the presence of language and hormones, the trans experience is a whirlwind of transformative energy that recodifies all political and cultural signifiers preventing a clear (cardinal, to use the medical terminology) delineation between yesterday and today, between the feminine and the masculine. I am the little girl who walks through a village in Cantabria, climbs cherry trees and scratches her legs. I am the boy who sleeps in the byre with the cows. I am the cow climbing the mountain slopes that hides from human eyes. I am Frankenstein's monster, carrying a flower and searching for someone to love while all around flee. I am the reader whose body becomes a book. I am the teenage boy kissing a girl behind the church door. I am the young girl who dresses up as a Jesuit and learns screeds of Spinoza's *Ethics* by heart. I am the skinhead lesbian going to seminars on BDSM at the Lesbian, Gay, Bisexual and Transgender Community Center on West 13th Street in Manhattan. I am the person who refuses to identify as a woman and who self-administers small doses of testosterone every day. I am an Orlando where writing has become chemistry. But I would like to avoid the heroic account of my transition. There was nothing heroic in it. I am not a werewolf and I do not possess the immortality of the vampire. The only thing that was heroic was the desire to live—the force with which the desire to change manifested, and still continues to manifest itself through me. Far from being particular, observations about my body and my personal trials and tribulations describe political ways of normalizing or deconstructing gender, sex and sexuality, and may therefore be of interest in forming a dissident knowledge opposed to the hegemonic languages of psychology, psychoanalysis and the neurosciences.

I am speaking about all of this publicly because it is vital that the voices of sexual and gender subalterns not be appropriated by the discourse of sexual difference. I know that I have turned my body into a showroom: but I would rather make of my life a literary legend, a biopolitical show, than allow psychiatry, pharmacology, psychoanalysis, medicine or the media to construct an image of me as an educated binary, integrationist homosexual or transsexual, as a sophisticated monster capable of expressing myself in the language of the norm, ladies and gentlemen, academics and psychoanalysts.

Medicine and the law of gender binarism portray the process of transsexuality as a narrow and dangerous path, a definitive, irreversible mutation, that can be achieved only in extreme conditions, such that few people, as few as possible, would be able to follow that path. I, however, would say that the path is easier and more pleasant than most of the experiences and experiments that the dominant discourse suggests are desirable and obligatory and which have been legitimized by medical and judicial institutions. In itself, gender transition is easier to accomplish than going to school every day at the same time throughout the long years of childhood and adolescence, easier than a faithful monogamous marriage, easier than pregnancy and childbirth, easier than starting a family, easier than finding a rewarding full-time job, easier than being happy in a consumer society, easier than growing old and being shut away in a retirement home. I would go so far as to say that, contrary to what is routinely claimed, the mutation process that accompanies gender transitioning is one of the most beautiful and joyous things that I have ever done in my life. All the things that are terrible and terrifying about transsexuality and gender transitioning are not found in the process of transition itself, but in the way in which the boundaries between the sexes punish and threaten to kill anyone who dares cross them. It is not gender transitioning that is horrifying and dangerous, but the regime of sexual difference.

Lastly, the process of transition that I am describing is in no sense irreversible. On the contrary, it would take only a conscious decision on my part to "re-identify" as a woman and a few months of not taking testosterone to be able to once again pass as a female body inhabiting the social space. The supposed unidirectionality of this journey is one of the normative lies in the history of psychiatry and psychoanalysis, one of the erroneous effects of binary thought. In a "trans" process, not only is it not necessary to become a man, it remains completely possible to once again "be" a woman, or indeed something completely different, if that were necessary or desirable.

To put it in the simplest possible terms: all of you here, eminent members of the École de la Cause Freudienne, could be homosexual or become "trans." Any one of you, anyone who deigned to dive into the kaleidoscope of their own desire and their own body, into their reservoir of nervous tension, into their own memory, might find an exhilarating excitement, a free energy that could lead them to live differently, to change, to be different, to be, so to speak, *radically alive*. The femininity or the masculinity you adopt and endorse is no less fabricated than mine. You would need only to review your history of normalization and submission to the dominant social and political codes of gender and sexuality in order to feel the spinning wheel of fabrication whirl inside you once more and with it the desire to break free of the repetition, to disidentify. To live beyond the patriarchal-colonial law, to live beyond the law of sexual difference, to live beyond sexual and gender violence is the right that every living body, even a psychoanalyst, should have.

But to place oneself, to live outside an epistemic and political regime, when a new cognitive framework, a new map of what it means to live, has not yet been collectively agreed is extremely difficult: in the process of transition, I did not reach the place where I set out to go. It is not easy to invent a new language, to invent all the terms of a new grammar. It is a vast, collective task. But however insignificant a single life might seem, no-one would dare say that the effort was not worthwhile.

However, if I, the monster, am here to address you today, ladies and gentlemen, practitioners and academics of the French school of psychoanalysis, it is not because I am interested in your views about my so-called "transsexuality." From my own personal experience, I can tell you that life is just as beautiful, perhaps more beautiful, that love is just as intense, perhaps more intense, when sexual difference and the forms of heterosexual and homosexual that you consider either normal or pathological are recognized for what they are: great fictional artifacts that we have collectively constructed and which, maybe once, who knows, were necessary to the survival of a certain group of human animals, and are now no more than an unwieldy armor that no longer results in anything other than death and oppression. Artifacts that were invented and politically legitimized, historical inventions, cultural conventions that have taken on the form of our bodies to such an extent that we identify with them. Normative masculinity and femininity, heterosexuality and homosexuality as conceived in the nineteenth century, are caught up in a process which, if it cannot be called disintegration, we must at least call deconstruction, through euphemism or philosophical conviction.

Allow me to take you on a little tour behind the scenes of this political edifice we call sexual difference, this collection of norms and power struggles which you may believe are indispensable conditions for life in society, but whose social enforcement has become untenable.

I simply want you to know, want everyone to know, through my personal experience, and through the accounts produced by sexual and gender subalterns, but also through scientific practice, precisely what is named by sexual difference. Thus enlightened, you can decide for yourselves.

And so that you can know and can decide, if you will permit me, with the unusual freedom conferred on me by the fact that I am addressing you from a discursive position as unexpected as it is impossible, that of a gender-dysphoric monster addressing the Academy of Psychoanalysts, I would like to pass at least three ideas to you today, for I have spent my whole life studying the different sexual and gender cages in which human beings imprison themselves.

I would like to begin by saying that the regime of sexual difference as promulgated by psychoanalysis is neither a nature nor a symbolic order but an epistemological politics of the body and that, as such, it is historical and changing.

Secondly, I would like to inform you, in case you did not already know, that this hierarchical epistemic binary regime has been in crisis since the 1940s, not just because of the challenges posed by the political movements of dissident minorities, but also because of the discovery of new data—morphological, chromosomal and biochemical—that renders sex and gender assignation at least contentious, if not impossible.

Thirdly, I would like to say that, shaken by profound changes, the epistemic regime of sexual difference is mutating and, within the next ten or twenty years, will probably give way to a new epistemology. Trans feminist, queer and anti-racist movements, together with new approaches to filiation, to loving relationships and to identification in terms of gender, desire, sexuality and naming, are merely signs of this mutation and of experiments in the collective construction of a different epistemology of the living human body.

Faced with the epistemological transformation already underway, you will have to decide, ladies and gentlemen, psychoanalysts of France, what you are going to do, where you intend to place yourselves, in which "cage" you would like to be imprisoned, and how you plan to play your discursive and clinical cards in a process as important as this.

I would ask for a few more minutes of your attention, that is if you can listen to a non-binary body and afford it the potential for reason and for truth.

I.

To begin with, the regime of sex, gender and sexual difference you consider universal and almost metaphysical, on which rests all psychoanalytical theory, is not an empirical reality, nor a determining symbolic order of the unconscious. It is no more than an epistemology of the living, an anatomical mapping, a political economy of the body and a collective administration of reproductive energies. A historic system of knowledge and representation constructed in accordance with a racial taxonomy during a period of European mercantile and colonial expansion that crystallized in the second half of the nineteenth century. Far from being a representation of reality, this epistemology is in fact a performative engine that produces and legitimizes a specific political and economic order: the hetero-colonial patriarchy.

When I talk about the regime of sex, gender and sexual difference as an epistemology, I am referring to a historical system of representations, a collection of discourses, institutions, conventions, practices and cultural agreements (be they symbolic, religious, scientific, technical, commercial or communicative) that make it possible for a society to decide what is true and to distinguish it from what is false, and, therefore, who should be considered human and under what conditions. To explain the workings of epistemological regimes, I will refer here to the studies on scientific paradigm shifts by the American philosopher of science Thomas Kuhn, and later developed by Ian Hacking, Bruno Latour and Donna Haraway.

A paradigm determines an order of the visible and the invisible, and as such brings with it an ontology and a political order, that is to say it establishes the difference between what exists and what does not exist socially and politically and establishes a hierarchy between different creatures. It establishes a specific means of experiencing reality through language, a collection of institutions that regulate the rituals of social production and reproduction. Bruno Latour reminds us that, despite the examples borrowed from Gestalt psychology, a paradigm is not a visual metaphor. A paradigm is not a simple world view. It is not an interpretation, much less a simple subjective representation. "It is the practice," Latour explains, "the modus operandi that allows new facts to emerge. It is more like a road that affords access to an experimental site than a filter that permanently colors the data. A paradigm acts rather like the runway of an airport. It makes it possible, in a manner of speaking, for certain facts to 'land.' It is easier to understand the importance Kuhn attaches to all the social, collective and institutional aspects of these paradigms. None of this matter, in his eyes, would weaken the truth and the commensurability of the sciences, nor their access to reality. On the contrary, if we focus on the material aspects that allow fact to 'land,' Kuhn argues, we would understand why progress in the sciences is so conservative, so slow, so viscous. Just as a hydroplane cannot land at Orly airport, so a quantum[2] cannot 'land' in Newton's physics."

An epistemology represents a closure of our cognitive system that not only offers answers to our questions, but determines the very questions that we can pose according to a pre-established interpretation of sensory data. Scientific paradigms are agreements shared by a social community which, though they do not have the status of self-evident or established axioms, are nonetheless so widely accepted that they become almost impossible to contest since they are used to solve all manner of problems. Paradigms are "discourse worlds" in which a certain coherence, a certain semio-technical peace, a certain agreement reign. But they are not worlds of immutable meaning. The distinctive characteristic of an epistemology is that it is flexible enough to allow for the resolution of a

2. In quantum mechanics, the quantum represents the smallest possible, and therefore indivisible, unit of a given quantity of energy, of mass or of movement. Quanta do not exist in Newtonian physics.

certain number of problems. Up to the point where the problems raised by an epistemology are more numerous than those they solve. At such a point, epistemology, by definition conservative, slow and viscous, becomes refractory, harmful, even deleterious until it is replaced by a new epistemology, a new mechanism capable of dealing with new questions.

We might therefore say that the regime of sex, gender and sexual difference is a historical epistemology, a cultural, techno-scientific paradigm that has not always existed and which is subject, like all epistemologies, to critique and to change. Contemporary historians of the science and society of the Renaissance now agree that until the Middle Ages and perhaps as late as the early seventeenth century, the dominant Western epistemology was the "one-sex model" in which only the male body was recognized as anatomically perfect. In the texts of Hippocrates and of Galen of Pergamon and the anatomical treatises of Andreas Vesalius, the bodies of women shared the same anatomy as those of men: only the absence of internal heat indicated that, in women, genital organs remained inside the body, whereas in men, the warmer and more perfect gender, the genital organs were externalized. People spoke of men and women, but also of angels and demons, monsters and chimeras. But in this epistemology, men and angels had greater ontological and political reality than women and chimeras. Before the nineteenth century, "woman" did not exist either anatomically or politically in terms of sovereign subjectivity. The mono-sexual paradigm operated according to a "system of similarities" in which the female body was represented as a hierarchically lesser variation of the male. The bodies of women were not recognized as anatomical entities, as political subjects, as possessing a full, autonomous ontological existence. Before the eighteenth century, a vagina was an inverted penis, the clitoris and the fallopian tubes did not exist, and the ovaries were internalized testicles. Gynecology was limited to obstetrics. There were no women. There were only potential mothers. Menstruation and the capacity for reproduction defined womanhood, not the form of the genital organs. Genitality as an anatomico-political indicator of sexual difference is a much more recent invention. In the patriarchal regime, only the male body and male sexuality were acknowledged as sovereign. The female body and female sexuality were subaltern, dependent, minor(itarian)—not in the numerical sense, obviously, but in the sense given by Deleuze and Guattari to the term, as a variable of subjugation in relations of power.

Throughout the eighteenth and nineteenth centuries, new medical and visual techniques gradually gave rise to an "aesthetics of anatomical difference" which opposes the anatomy of the penis with that of the vagina; the ovaries with the testicles; the production of sperm and uterine reproduction; chromosomes X and Y; but also the male productive work to female reproductive domesticity. A new binary epistemology that rests on a "system of oppositions" between the sexes is established through the biological treatises of Carl Linnaeus, Georges Cuvier and Georges de Buffon, the genetic theories of Hermann Henking (who "discovered" and named the "X chromosome" in 1891), the writings on obstetrics by Alfred Louis Velpeau and Charles Clay, and the colonial gynecology of J. Marion Sim.[3]

Various historians of science have studied the process of change and transition that led from a one-sex paradigm to the paradigm of sexual difference. According to Thomas Laqueur, it was a brutal change that took place in the eighteenth century

---

3. In 2017, the anti-racist collective "Black Youth Project 100" staged a protest in front of the statue of J. Marion Sim in Central Park opposite the New York Academy of Medicine. J. Marion Sim bought Black female slaves on whom he performed gynecological experiments, including vivisection and sterilization.

and coincided with the growing political emancipation of women's bodies. However, according to the historian Helen King, there was no abrupt shift from one epistemology to the other, instead she argues that throughout antiquity and into the Renaissance the one-sex model never succeeded in completely dominating the anatomico-political epistemology, and co-existed with a semi-emergent two-sex model which eventually came to predominate at the end of the eighteenth century. Despite differences in their methodologies and analyses, most historians agree that, in the late eighteenth century, the invention of an aesthetics of anatomical difference served to shore up the political ontology of the patriarchy by establishing "natural" differences between men and women at a time when the universalization on a one-sex model could have been used to justify women's access to the mechanics of government and to political life.

It is interesting to think that Freudian psychoanalysis, both as a theory of the psychic apparatus and as clinical practice, was invented at precisely the moment when the ideas central to the epistemology of racial and sexual difference were crystallized: evolved races and primitive races, man and woman defined as anatomically different and complementary by virtue of their reproductive power, as potential paternal or maternal figures respectively in the bourgeois colonial institution of the family; but also heterosexuality and homosexuality respectively considered as normal and pathological. Seen through the lens of the history of vile bodies, of the history of monsters and their relationship with normative sexuality, psychoanalysis is the science of the patriarchal-colonial unconscious, the theory of the unconscious of sexual difference.

Psychoanalysis does not merely work in and with this epistemology of sexual difference, in fact, if I may be so bold, it was crucial in the subjugation and the creation of the female and male "psyches," together with the heterosexual and homosexual typologies that form the main axes of the patriarchal-colonial regime. The epistemology of sex, gender and sexual difference is not external to psychoanalysis: it is the inherent and immanent condition on which the whole psychoanalytic theory of sexuality is based. Psychoanalytic concepts of the libido, of active-passive roles, penis envy, castration anxiety, the phallic woman, genital love, hysteria, masochism, bisexuality, androgyny, the phallic phase, the Oedipus complex, the oedipal position, the pre-genital and genital stages, perversion, coitus, the preliminary pleasure principle, the primal scene, homosexuality, heterosexuality—the list is almost endless—are meaningless outside the epistemology of sex, gender and sexual difference.

With the invention of new secular and sanitized methods of accessing the living body (i.e. freed from the rituals of touch and of blood), to that "invisible" and "untouchable" part of the living body that psychoanalysis calls the "unconscious," "the talking cure" succeeds in doing something that no other institution within the regime of sex, gender and sexual difference can do: devise a language of sexuality, instill a feeling of normal and pathological sexual identity and gender identity, offer a patriarchal and colonial meaning to dreams, and gradually form a kernel of binary identity based on autofiction.

I would ask you, please, not to attempt to deny the complicity of psychoanalysis in the heteronormative epistemology of sex, gender and sexual difference. I am offering you the possibility of an epistemological critique of your psychoanalytic theories, a political therapy for your institutional practices. But such processes cannot take place without an exhaustive critique of your presuppositions. Don't repress them, don't deny them, don't stifle them, don't displace them.

Don't tell me that sex, gender and sexual difference is not crucial in explaining the structure of the psychic apparatus in psychoanalysis. The entire Freudian edifice is conceived from the position of patriarchal masculinity, from the heterosexual male body seen as a body with an erect penis, penetrating and ejaculating; this is why "women" in psychoanalysis, those strange creatures (sometimes) equipped with a reproductive uterus and clitoris, remain and will remain a problem. This is why, in 2019, you still feel the need to set aside a day to talk about "women in psychoanalysis."

Don't tell me that the psychoanalytic institution has not considered homosexuality to be a deviation from the norm: how else can you explain why, until very recently, there were no psychoanalysts who could publicly identify themselves as homosexual? Let me ask: how many of you here today, in the École de la Cause Freudienne, publicly identify as psychoanalysts and homosexuals?[4]

Silence? No-one has anything to say?

Panic in the lecture hall. Epistemic terror on the analyst's couch.

I am not forcing the disclosure of subjective private positions, but the acknowledgement of a political enunciation within the regime of colonial hetero-

---

4. The silence of the lecture hall is broken only by scattered laughter and booing.

patriarchal power. Contrary to what is stated or affirmed by psychoanalysis, I do not believe that heterosexuality is a sexual practice or a sexual identity but, like Monique Wittig, a political regime that reduces the sum total of the living human body and its psychic energy to its reproductive potential, a position of discursive and institutional power. Epistemologically and politically, the psychoanalyst is a binary heterosexual body…until proven otherwise.

I am not asking homosexual psychoanalysts to come out of the closet. It is heteronormative psychoanalysts who urgently need to come out of the closet of the norm.

In the late nineteenth century, Freudian psychoanalysis began to function as a technology for regulating the psychic apparatus "enclosed" within the patriarchal and colonial epistemology of sex, gender and sexual difference. Today, Freud is recognized as among the most important thinkers of modern times, on a level with Nietzsche or Marx. But like those of Nietzsche or Marx, his discursive elaborations need to be questioned and critiqued in the light of new processes of political emancipation and techno-scientific transformation. I don't think I am divulging a secret when I say that Freudian psychoanalysis has placed the normalization of heterosexual femininity and masculinity at the center of the clinical narrative, together with the desire and the authority of the father. A feminist and queer rereading of the Freudian Oedipus complex is urgently needed. I cannot engage in hermeneutics of his texts here, but, briefly, I can say that in placing the blame on Oedipus and putting all the weight of the analysis on his supposed "incestuous desire," Freud and normative psychoanalysis have contributed to the enduring nature of patriarchal domination by making the victim responsible for the rape and transforming into psychological law the social rituals of the normalization of gender, and of the sexual violence and abuse of children and women that underpins patriarchal-colonial culture.

In Freudian psychoanalysis there is no attempt to overcome the heteronormative epistemology of sexual difference and binary gender, but rather there is the development of a technology, a collection of discursive and therapeutic practices to "normalize" the positions of "man" and "woman" and their dominant or deviant colonial sexual identifications. One might say that the contemporary patriarchal-colonial subject expends most of their psychic energy producing a normative binary identity: anxiety, hallucination, melancholy, depression, dissociation, opacity, repetition...are only the psychological and social costs that result from the dual extraction process of the force of production and the force of reproduction. Psychoanalysis is not a critique of this epistemology, but the therapy needed for the patriarchal-colonial subject to continue to function despite the extraordinary psychic cost and the inexpressible violence of this regime. Faced with depoliticized psychoanalysis, we would need a radically political approach that begins with the depatriarchalization and decolonization of the body and the psychic apparatus.

I speak with no animosity. I myself underwent psychoanalysis for seventeen years with various analysts, Freudian, Kleinian, Lacanian, Guattarian… Everything I express here, I do so not as an "outsider," but as a body of psychoanalysis, a monster of the analyst's couch.

To begin with, it would be impossible for me to qualify my multiple experiences of analysis with a single adjective, either good or bad. The success or failure of my analytic sessions largely depended not on the fidelity of the analysts to Freud, Klein or Lacan, but, on the contrary, to their infidelity, or, to put it another way, on their creativity, their ability to step outside the "cage." Over the course of different sessions, I was able to observe how my analysts had to struggle with, and against, the theoretical framework in which they had been trained in order to be able to listen to a non-binary "trans" person without bringing up diagnosis, critique, conversion or cure. In certain cases, my cure depended precisely on my ability to escape the psychoanalytic norm, as when I left in the middle of a session during which the analyst had done everything possible to rid me of what he considered "the multiple forms of fetishism that threatened my female sexuality." To me, what the analyst saw as deviant fetishes were fundamental experiments towards defining a new epistemology of sexual being, beyond the dichotomy of man-woman, penis-vagina, penetrator-penetrated. In other cases, I was able to make part of the journey in the company of psychoanalysts I would describe as dissident in practice, but silent and discreet in theory. I would like to think that most of the psychoanalysts who are here today and listening to me are part of that silent, potentially revolutionary group. It is to you, in the first instance, that I address myself.

No-one is required to be faithful to the mistakes of the past. Neither you nor anyone else. I am not denouncing the misogyny of Freud here, or the racism and transphobia of Lacan. What I am denouncing is the fidelity of psychoanalysis, developed over the course of the twentieth century, to the epistemology of sex, gender and sexual difference and to dominant Western colonial reason. This is not a problem that can be solved by the good intentions of an individual, just as the good intentions of Bartolomé de las Casas were not enough to overcome the racist epistemology and colonial political practices that led to the extermination of indigenous populations in the Americas.

Lastly, I wanted to say that the unease you feel when you hear me speak, the irrepressible urge to repudiate my words, the urgent desire to explain away what I am saying by relating to my apparent condition as "gender dysphoric" is part and parcel of the crisis you feel at the epistemological controversy raging through contemporary psychoanalysis. This crisis is vital; it is constructive.

II.

The uncritical use of the epistemology of sex, gender and sexual difference by Freudian psychoanalysis entered into crisis after the Second World War. Those who found themselves reduced by this epistemology to abject subjects, to objects of knowledge, to monsters began to rise up and found new ways to make their voices heard: movements campaigning for women's reproductive and political sovereignty over their own bodies, for the depathologizing of homosexuality, for trans people to have access to medical and administrative services, together with the invention of new techniques in the representation and manipulation of the biochemical structures of the living body (chromosome mapping, prenatal diagnosis, hormone administration, etc.) led to a situation that was unprecedented in the 1940s.

Medical and psychiatric discourse seems to have mounting problems in dealing with the appearance of bodies that cannot immediately be assigned female or male at birth. Beginning in 1940, new chromosomal and endocrinological techniques, together with the medicalization of childbirth, led to the diagnosis of an increasing number of babies as what used to be termed "hermaphrodite." Confronted by these newborns, now referred to as "intersex," the medical scientific community devised a new taxonomy. John Money, a child psychologist working at Johns Hopkins University with Lawson Wilkins, the founder of pediatric endocrinology, sets aside the modern notion of "sex" as an anatomical reality and invents the notion of "gender" to talk about the possibility of using technology to create sexual difference. The modern notion of transsexuality also first appears in this context between 1947 and 1960.

In 1966, the Swiss pediatrician Andrea Prader devises and introduces a clinical scale for determining gender using the "orchidometer" also known as "Prader's balls" or the "endocrine rosary"—a string of twenty-five numbered beads of various sizes that can be used, according to Prader, to measure the virilization of the testicles in prepubertal children. Paradoxically, his belief in the "normality" of binarism and his obsession with taxonomy lead Prader to highlight twenty-five different types of testicular morphology. His "orchidometer" could be seen as proof of the multiplicity of morphological variants in the living body… But, unable to overcome the epistemology of sex, gender and sexual difference, Prader considers most of these differences to be "pathologies" and recommends a whole battery of therapies designed to allow for gender reassignment. For the first time, medicine and psychiatry discover to their horror the existence of a multiplicity of bodies and genital morphologies beyond the binary. An increasing number of scientific, social and political controversies ensues. But instead of changing the epistemology, they decide to modify the body, to normalize sexualities, to rectify identifications.

I would like to share with you a hypothesis that all of Lacanian psychoanalysis, which is developed in the early 1950s—Lacan's rereading of Freud, his detour through linguistics—is an early response to the crisis in the epistemology of sex, gender and sexual difference. I believe it is possible to say that Lacan, like John Money, is trying to denaturalize sexual difference, but, just like Money, he eventually produces a metasystem that is almost more rigid than the modern notions of sex and anatomical difference. In Money's case, this metasystem introduces a grammar of gender considered as a construct of social indoctrination and endocrinology. With Lacan, too, the metasystem is not anatomical, it takes the form of the unconscious structured as a language, between the "Symbolic," "Imaginary" and "Real" orders... But, as in the case of John Money, while it is not reduced to anatomy, it is a system of differences that does not go beyond sexual binarism and the patriarchal genealogy of language. My hypothesis is that Lacan fails to break free of sex, gender and sexual binarism because of his own position within the heterosexual patriarchate as political regime. His denaturalization was conceptually operational, but Lacan himself was not politically ready. And so, psychoanalysis, both Freudian and Lacanian, forcefully contributed to the normalization of non-conforming bodies as "intersex," and the pathologizing of non-binary and trans identities as "transsexuality."

Please do not think, after my detour via Freud and Lacan, that it is easy for me to present myself as a "transsexual" before an assembly of psychoanalysts. Any more than it must have been easy for Red Peter, the ape who escaped the music hall to became a man, however free he was, however far from his chains, to speak before an assembly of scientists, vets and animal tamers, however benevolent and reformist, despite the flowers and the piano on the stage. The practices of observation, objectification, punishment, exclusion and death put in place by psychoanalysis and psychiatry when dealing with dissidents to the regimes of sexual difference and colonial heteropatriarchy, with individuals considered as "homosexuals," with men or women who have been raped or sexually abused, with sex workers, with trans people, with racialized people, are perhaps less spectacular than those of the circus or the zoo, but no less efficient.

I do not believe the comparison is gratuitous, not simply because as homosexuals, transsexuals, sex workers, racialized, transvestite or non-binary bodies we too have been othered and animalized, but because what medicine, psychiatry and psychoanalysis have done to sexual minorities over the course of the past two centuries is a comparable process of institutional and political extermination.

On the one hand, the majority of those who refused to live according to the patriarchal norms of sexual difference were persecuted by the police and the judicial system as potentially criminal, and on the other, they were pathologized by the psychiatric and psychoanalytical framework, locked in psychiatric prisons, raped in order to prove their true "femininity" or "masculinity," subjected to lobotomies, hormone therapy, electroconvulsive therapy or the so-called "analytical cure." When dealing with us, the monsters of patriarchal-colonial modernity, talking cures and behavioral or pharmacological therapies were not in open conflict, they worked in a complementary fashion. A process of political extermination of the dissident minorities of the regime of sex, gender and sexual difference was at work. Many of my predecessors died and continue to die to this day, murdered, raped, beaten, incarcerated, medicalized...or they lived or are living their difference in secret. This is my heritage, and it is with the strength that I draw from all their silenced voices, though in my own name only, that I address you today.

The terminological abuse to which the word "transsexual" would be subjected—the word that some of those present would use to describe me today—began in the 1950s with David Oliver Cauldwell, Harry Benjamin and Robert Stoller, at precisely the same time that Lacan was developing his psychoanalytic theories, but the epistemic persecution and genocide began much earlier, in the late nineteenth century, with Karl Friedrich Otto Westphal's characterization of certain subjects who "suffered" from what he called "contrary sexual feeling." For Westphal, there was no difference between what we now call "homosexuality" and "transsexuality"; what mattered was the difference between natural desire and that which was against nature. Seen from the perspective of a rigid binary regime, the problem was "inversion," the stubborn determination to "imitate" the practices of the "other sex." In the nineteenth century, it was thought that homosexuality was in fact caused by the "migration" of a female soul into a male body, or vice versa. All regimes are policed by borders, thus migration continues to cause problems to this day, whether practiced between bodies and souls or between nation states. As a result, having adopted a reproductive heterosexual model requiring bio-penis/bio-vagina penetration and insemination, psychology depicted male homosexuals as effeminate men of passive or receptive anal sexuality, for example; meanwhile, lesbians were conceived as masculine women of phallic or active sexuality.

The German psychopathologist Richard von Krafft-Ebing categorized a sphere of "sexual inversion" in which those who wish to live as I do now were considered abnormal: "psychical hermaphrodites" or patients suffering from "metamorphosis sexualis paranoica" long before the term "transsexual" was invented. The theory of homosexuality as sexual inversion would be replaced in the late 1940s by Alfred Kinsey, who, for the first time, defines homosexuality as sexual relations between two people of the same sex.

It is at the point when the representations of homosexuality and heterosexuality are changing that Cauldwell uses the term "psychopathic trans-sexual" to characterize "an individual who is unfavorably affected [who] psychologically determines to live and appear as a member of the sex to which he or she does not belong." Despite the fact that the first "sex-change" operations had been performed in the 1930s, Cauldwell, who advocates "treating the mind, not the body," opposes all bodily transformation. At the same time the child psychiatrist John Money considers that transsexuals suffer from a "gender identity disorder" since they manifest an "irrational desire to live as the other sex."

The terminological abuse continues: in 1973, Norman Fisk introduces the term "gender dysphoria," which would eventually be included as a pathological characterization of transsexuality in the *Diagnostic and Statistical Manual of Mental Disorders (DSM)*. The shift from traditional psychiatry to the DSM also marks a shift in the language from mental illness and insanity towards "behavioral disorders," and the progressive shift from external practices of institutionalization and surveillance towards new biochemical and pharmacological techniques to produce and control subjectivity. Still obsessed with the gradations between the normal and the pathological and by the difference between anatomical reality and the practice of gender, Henry Benjamin, Robert Stoller and Norman Fisk created the basis for the absurd taxonomies still used to describe us: the difference between transvestism, considered merely a desire to pass oneself off as the opposite sex by the use of clothing, and "real" transsexuality as a corporeal metamorphosis that, for Stoller, entails a series of hormonal and surgical interventions.

Similarly, in 1987, the American sexologist Ray Blanchard leads a "scientific" campaign to have a typology entered into the DSM that would make it possible to distinguish between various degrees of pathology among "transvestites" and "transsexual women." His controversial theory posited links between gender performance, homosexual and heterosexual desires and transsexuality. It is still used by numerous therapists and is known as "Blanchard's transsexualism typology."

The idea that a transsexual person must necessarily be heterosexual, together with the grotesque, insistent question "Post-op trans or pre-op trans?" that some of you are doubtless asking yourselves as you listen to me, are the result of the psychopathological framework.

Allow me to reassure you: I have had surgery; carefully, over the course of lengthy political, practical and theoretical sessions, I surgically removed the epistemic apparatus that diagnoses my body and my behaviors as pathological.

What of you, esteemed psychoanalysts, have you had surgery?

The increasing politicization of trans and intersex movements since the 1990s, something that has intensified over the course of the past decade, has led to a shift in the idea of "gender dysphoria" towards one of "gender identity disorder." The struggle for depathologization continues, but what is at stake is not merely the depathologization of so-called "trans identity": a whole epistemology needs to be changed.

In this, psychoanalysis is no better than pediatrics or pharmacological psychiatry. While you may have opposed the medicalization of neurosis and the transformation of the patient into a consumer of psychotropic drugs using new cognitive-behavioral therapies (CBT), you have never denied yourself the right to intervene in the normalization of homosexuality and transsexuality, and the psychoanalytical management of gender and sexual deviancy.

For Lacan, transsexuals are psychotic, victims of an error of "mistaking the organ for the signifier." It is possible to get rid of the organ, but it is impossible to get rid of the symbolic "signifier" of sexuation which, according to him, divides all creatures into male and female. As trans people, he claims, we suffer from a semiotic illness: we don't understand the difference between symbolic castration and real castration, between a vagina and a simple orifice, between a "phallus" and some random fleshy appendage; we just don't get it. But does the medical profession make a distinction between a vagina and a simple orifice, between a "phallus" and a random appendage when, looking at an ultrasound or during a birth, it assigns gender? What if the epistemology of sex, gender and sexual difference in itself were a pathology of the signifier?

Esteemed Lacanian psychoanalysts, one does not need to soar to the heady heights of the Symbolic Order to come to the same conclusion as Catholic Spanish nationalist groups when they say: "Don't let yourself be fooled: a boy has a penis. A girl has a vulva." It does not matter whether you designate the penis and the vulva as signifiers of sexuation, or as mere organs. What if it were not clear-cut that there are only penises and the vulvas? What if there were girls with penises and boys with vulvas? What if there were more than two sexes, more than two genders, more than two core sexual orientations? What if genital difference or gender expression were not the criteria for the acceptance of a human body in a social and political collective?

Here lies the complexity and the challenge of trans and intersex experience. But psychoanalysis prefers to pathologize rather than question the paradigm of sex, gender and sexual difference. In 1983, to acclaim from *Le Monde*, the psychoanalyst and last partner of Jacques Lacan, Catherine Millot, published *Horsexe*, an essay on transsexuality, in which she asserted her belief that any attempt at sex and gender transition is a desperate and psychotic attempt at pushing back the frontiers of reality (the real). She describes the trans body as hideous and grotesque, an absurd and monstrous incarnation that only someone who was mentally ill could prefer to their own "healthy," "original" body. "The man who dreams of being a trans woman," Millot asserts, "must be confronted with the drama of real castration." Meanwhile the castration of our freedoms carries on unhindered. In the works of Janine Chasseguet-Smirgel, the desire of trans people to change their physical appearance stems from a failure to resolve the Oedipus complex, and the perverse propensity to regress to the pregenital state. More recently, in 2003, the psychoanalyst Colette Chiland asserted that, faced with the impossibility of overcoming the reality of the sex and gender binary, transsexuals present a "borderline state," that leads them to lapse into pathology akin to "narcissistic fantasy." Following on from the work of André Green, Chiland considers gender reassignment surgery to be "self-mutilation," or a "private madness" that becomes "collective madness" when accepted by doctors.

The "transsexual patient," according to Chiland, represents an "insoluble problem" for the psychoanalyst. First and foremost, Chiland says, "transsexual patients" are not amenable to analytical transference because, according to her, they cannot feel castration anxiety, nor do they feel empathy towards the analyst. In fact, according to Chiland, it is the psychoanalyst who treats "a trans-sexual patient" who suffers the effects of transference: the male analyst faced with a man who wishes to become a woman, physically suffers castration anxiety when he hears his patient talk about wanting to get rid of his penis; meanwhile the female analyst, according to Chiland, will listen in horror to the desire of a woman (a trans person whom Chiland considers to be a woman) who wishes to get rid of her breasts, since this desire, according to the psychoanalyst, will negate her own physical and erotic experience of the breast. In fact, the physical, erotic and sexual experiences of the trans person trigger an irrepressible anxiety in the analyst. As such, it is perhaps not the trans person who refuses to engage with the analytic process, but rather the analyst who cannot face the challenge of looking at a body beyond his/her cisgender heterosexual experience and sexual conventions.

For Lacan and his supporters, sexual binarism is a symbolic fact and a bodily aesthetic as irrefutable as the sun revolving around the earth for Ptolemy. It is possible to get rid of the organ but, for psychoanalysis, it is impossible to get rid of the patriarchal-colonial epistemology of sexual difference. To extend Bruno Latour's argument about the power of the paradigm, one might say that it is more difficult for a non-binary body to exist on the psychoanalyst's couch than it is for a hydroplane to land at Orly, or a quantum to "land" in Newtonian physics.

III.

But, beginning in 1950, with the gradual emancipation of heterosexual women, the depathologization of homosexuality, the commercialization of the contraceptive pill and the increased public visibility of non-binary gender positions, the epistemology of sex, gender and sexual difference is subjected to an inexorable process of re-examination. These political challenges are further intensified by a scientific controversy prompted by new chromosomal or biochemical "data" derived from enhanced techniques for mapping chromosomes and genomes, or endocrine diagnostics.

In 1993, a group of patients set up the Intersex Society of North America (ISNA) to publicize their struggle against the medicalization and the surgical modification of their bodies without their consent. In the same year, Anne Fausto-Sterling, Professor of Biology and Gender Studies at Brown University, publishes a much-debated article in which she proposes moving from the binary epistemology to one that includes at least five sexes in order to respect the bodily integrity of those with morphological or genetic variations. In the years that followed, trans movements would push for the depathologization of transsexuality and demand the right to choose whether the process of gender transition necessarily entailed hormonal and surgical modifications, or merely a change in naming.

From 2010, the World Health Organization (WHO)—hardly an organization one could reasonably suspect of being complicit with radical feminist hypotheses, queer or trans theories—begins to nuance its position about the existence of variations in the morphological, anatomical and chromosomal reality of human bodies that goes beyond the sexual and the gender binary.

Today, it is the WHO, not some Anarcho-Feminist TransQueerDyke association, that asserts that "Gender, typically described in terms of masculinity and femininity, is a social construction that varies across different cultures and over time." And it recognizes that there were, and still are, certain cultures (Samoa in the Pacific, the First Peoples of the Americas, traditional Thai culture) that use taxonomies of sex and gender that are non-binary, more fluid and more complex than the modern Western taxonomy promulgated since the 1970s. In accepting the viability of non-pathological variations in the physical embodiments and social expressions of gender and sexuality, the WHO acknowledges the arbitrary and non-natural dimension of the binary taxonomy used by social and political institutions in the West, and opens the door not only to a reformulation of its terms, but also to a more profound reconsideration of the paradigm of sex, gender and sexual difference.

Today, we know that one out of 1,000–1,500 newborns (or six babies a day in the United States) that cannot be assigned within the gender binary are identified as "intersex." Over the course of the past twenty years, those children who were medicalized or underwent surgery because they were "intersex" rallied to demand an end to genital mutilations and the process of forced reassignment. Over the same period, more and more people begin to define themselves as "non-binary." A few months ago, the eminent philosopher Judith Butler legally registered themself with the State of California as a non-binary person. Various American states, and also Argentina and Australia, legally recognize non-binary gender as a political possibility. Germany has just recognized a third sex (O) as a possible gender assignation.

Simultaneously, a new distinction has been introduced between "cis" persons (those who identify with the sex assigned to them at birth) and "trans" persons (those who do not identify with that assignation and choose to transition, identifying either as trans or as non-binary).

Gender transition and the assertion of non-binary gender have thrown not only normative notions of what is male and what is female into crisis, but also the heterosexual and homosexual categories used by normative psychoanalysis and psychology. When the diagnosis of gender dysphoria is rejected, when the possibility of a social and sexual life beyond binary difference is asserted, definitions of homosexuality and heterosexuality, active and passive sexual roles, penetrator and penetrated, also become obsolete.

Moreover, the designation of heterosexuality as the only normal reproductive sexuality together with patriarchal depictions of fatherhood and biopolitical depictions of motherhood seem increasingly anachronistic when faced with the many possible ways of managing reproduction, and assisted pro-creation: the contraceptive pill, the morning-after pill, trans paternity, ART, surrogacy, and research projects in womb transplant, the possibility of creating artificial wombs, etc.

I don't know how to summon the enthusiasm, the urgency to tell you that we are living through a period of unprecedented historic importance: the epistemology of sex, gender and sexual difference is mutating.

In years to come, we will have to collectively devise an epistemology capable of taking into account the radical diversity of living beings, one that does not relegate the body to its capacity for heterosexual reproduction, one that does not legitimize hetero-patriarchal and colonial violence.

You are free to decide whether or not you believe me, but believe this at least: life is mutation and multiplicity. You need to understand that the future monsters are also your children and your grandchildren.

We are witnessing a process of transformation in the order of sexual and political anatomy comparable to that which led from the geocentric epistemo-logy of Ptolemy to the heliocentric epistemology of Copernicus. Or the transition, between 1650 and 1870, from the one-sex model to the anato-my of sexual difference. Or the paradigm shift introduced in the early twentieth century by relativity and quantum physics in comparison to Newtonian physics.

The process leading to an epistemological change will result in profound technological, social, visual and sensorial changes. For example, the changes that led from geocentrism and Aristotelian physics to heliocentrism and Newtonian physics coincided with the invention of the printing press and the steam engine. Printing hastened the shift from an oral culture to one based on reading and writing, together with the gradual secularization of biblical texts, and accelerated the process of European expansion and colonial expropriation in the Americas. The development of modern science, the institutional normalization of the heterosexual family and the expansion of the global market were accompanied by a biopolitics of national identity involving class divisions, sexual hierarchies, racial segregation and ethnic cleansing.

It is the integrated global capitalist regime, to paraphrase Félix Guattari, that we are in the process of abandoning. The economic, political and technological changes that led to the regime of sex, gender and sexual difference and colonial capitalism occurred over three centuries, but the speed of technological changes and the urgent need for political decisions in the face of the destruction of the ecosystem and the Anthropocene extinction means that we are faced with more rapid, perhaps imminent changes. Meanwhile, the internet, quantum physics, biotechnology, the robotization of work, artificial intelligence, genetic engineering, new technologies for assisted repro-duction and extra-terrestrial travel are hastening unprecedented changes requiring the invention of alternative modalities of existence between organism and machine, living and non-living, the human and the non-human, even as new hierarchies in the political sphere appear and disappear. A paradigm shift comparable to that wrought in the early twentieth century by quantum mechanics and the theories of relativity is now taking place in the techniques of procreating life and in the collective production of sexual and gender subjectivity.

This epistemic crisis has seen a resurgence in the politics of renaturalization, discursive regression and cognitive obstruction. As Kuhn taught us, for as long as one paradigm shift is not replaced by another, the accumulated unresolved problems do not, paradoxically, lead to reassessment or to lucid criticism, but rather to a temporary "rigidification" and a "hyperbolic affirmation" of the theoretical hypotheses of the paradigm under attack. It may even be possible to explain the current hyperbolic presentation of patriarchal-colonial ideologies and their populist and neo-nationalist power structures as a reaffirmation of the old paradigm, a denial of the epistemic crisis, a resistance to the mutation.

The new totalitarianism of sex, gender and sexual difference may delay epistemic collapse, but it cannot prevent it. This paradigm shift may mark the passage from sex, gender and sexual difference (a binary opposition, whether considered as dialectical or complementary, as duality or duel) to an endless number of differences of bodies, of unidentified and unidentifiable desires. We are not calling for the suppression of differences, for a return to the pre-modern one-sex model, whether female, male or neuter, nor for a homogenous unitary sexuality, nor for a simple reversal of hierarchies. Rather, we are talking about a proliferation of practices and forms of life, a multiplication of desires capable of unfurling beyond genital pleasure.

When I talk about a new epistemology, I am not referring simply to the transformation of scientific and technical practices, but rather a radical broadening of the democratic horizon to recognize all living bodies as political subjects without such social and political recognition being contingent on a sexual or gender assignation. It is the epistemic violence of the paradigm of sex, gender and sexual difference and the patriarchal-colonial regime that is being challenged by the feminist, anti-racist, intersex, trans and crip-queer movements demanding that those who were branded political subaltern be recognized as living bodies with full rights.

In the context of epistemic transition, you, the esteemed members of the l'Académie de Psychanalyse de France and the École de la Cause Freudienne, have an onerous responsibility. It is up to you to decide whether you wish to remain on the side of patriarchal and colonial discourse and to reassert the universality of sex, gender and sexual difference and heterosexual reproduction, or whether you wish to join us, the mutants and the monsters of this world, in a process of criticism and invention of a new epistemology that will allow for the redistribution of sovereignty and the recognition of other forms of political subjectivity.

You can no longer systematically appeal to the texts of Freud or Lacan as though they have a universality beyond a historically situated value system, as though these texts were not written from within the patriarchal epistemology of sex, gender and sexual difference. To hold up Freud and Lacan as law is as absurd as asking Galileo to revert to Ptolemy's model, as demanding that Einstein abandon relativity and carry on thinking in terms of Newtonian and Aristotelian physics.

Today, the once monstrous bodies produced by the patriarchal-colonial regime of sex, gender and sexual difference speak for themselves and produce knowledges about themselves. A raft of movements—queer, transfeminist, indigenous, #MeToo, #NiUnaMenos, Handi, Crip-Queer, #BlackLivesMatter, #BlackTransLivesMatter—are making decisive changes. You cannot carry on talking about the Oedipus complex or the name of the father in a society in which, for the first time in history, their legacy of femicide is acknowledged, in which the victims of patriarchal violence are speaking out to denounce their fathers, their husbands, their bosses, their boyfriends; in which women are denouncing the institutionalized politics of rape, in which thousands of bodies take to the streets to condemn homophobic attacks and the almost daily murders of trans women, together with all forms of institutionalized racism. You can no longer continue to assert the universality of sex and gender difference and the immutability of heterosexual and homosexual identities in a society where it is legal to change gender or to identify as gender non-binary, in a society where thousands of children have already been born to non-heterosexual and non-binary families. To continue to practice psychoanalysis with clinical tools like the Oedipus complex is as absurd as claiming to navigate the universe using a Ptolemaic geocentric map, as denying climate change, or asserting that the earth is flat.

We do not simply reject the patriarchal and sexual practices of kinship and binary heterocentric socialization. We reject your epistemology, and we must do so forcefully. Our position is one of epistemological insubordination.

Today, it is more important for psychoanalysts such as you to listen to the voices of bodies excluded by the patriarchal-colonial regime than to reread Freud and Lacan. Stop hiding behind the skirts of the fathers of psychoanalysis. Your political duty is to take care of children, not to legitimize the violence of the patriarchal-colonial regime.

The time has come to drag the analysts' couches into the streets and collectivize speech, politicize bodies, debinarize gender and sexuality and decolonize the unconscious.

Set Oedipus free, join the monsters, do not hide patriarchal violence behind the so-called incestuous desire of children, and place at the heart of your clinical practice the bodies and the voices—his, hers and *their*—of those who have overcome rape and patriarchal violence, of those who already live beyond the patriarchal nuclear family, beyond heterosexuality and sexual difference, and of those—he, she and *they*—who are searching for and creating a way out.

Soon, we may face a new necropolitical alliance between the colonial patriarchate and new pharmacopornographic technologies. There is no doubt that we are already facing an increasing pharmacolization of so-called "psychiatric pathologies," a commercialization of health care industries, a computerization of the brain and a semio-informatic roboticization of subjectivity production techniques via Facebook, Instagram, Tinder, etc. But the dangers and the excesses represented by this proliferation of new techniques designed to control and to increase segmentation of the human animal cannot be used as an excuse by psychoanalysis for failing to re-evaluate its own categories.

My aim is not to hasten the downfall of psycho-analysis to further the rise of neuroscience, or, still less, of pharmacology. My mission is the revenge of the psychoanalytic and psychiatric "object" (in equal measure) over the institutional, clinical and micropolitical systems that shore up the violence wreaked by the sexual, gender and racial norms. We urgently need clinical practice to transition. This cannot happen without a revolutionary muta-tion in psychoanalysis, and a critical challenge of its patriarchal-colonial presuppositions. A transi-tion in clinical practice would entail a shift in position: the object of study becomes the subject, while the person who, until now, has been the subject agrees to submit to a process of study, questioning and experimentation. The former sub-ject agrees to change. The subject/object duality (both clinically and epistemologically) disappears and is replaced by a new relationship, one that conjointly leads to mutation and to becoming other. It will be about strength and mutation rather than power and knowledge. It will entail learning together, and healing our wounds, aban-doning the techniques of violence and devising a new approach to the reproduction of life on a planetary scale.

Psychoanalysis is faced with a historic choice that is without precedent: either it continues to work with the old epistemology of sex, gender and sexual difference, offering de facto legitimacy to the patriarchal-colonial regime that underpins it, and thus becomes responsible for the acts of violence it begets, or it opens itself up to a political critique of its discourse and its practices.

The latter option entails initiating a process of depatriarchalization, deheterosexualization and decolonization of psychoanalysis, as discourse, as narrative, as institution and as clinical practice. Psychoanalysis must engage with critical feedback from Black, queer, feminist, and trans political traditions if it wishes to stop being a tool for heteropatriarchal normalization and the legitimizing of necropolitical violence, to become a tool for the invention of subjectivities that are dissident to the norm.

I appear before you today not to accuse, but rather to warn of the epistemological violence of the binary regime and to seek a new paradigm.

Psychoanalysts in favor of epistemic transition, join us! Together let us create a way out!

Contrary to the fears of the most conservative among you that psychoanalysis stripped of the epistemology of sex, gender and sexual difference would be disfigured, I say that only through such a profound transition can psychoanalysis survive.

And I say this from my position as a trans man, a non-binary body who has had to transform in order to leave his former "cage" and to survive by discovering, precariously, day by day, other paths to freedom. If I contemplate my evolution and its current outcome, I can neither complain, nor can I feel satisfied. There is still too much to do.

I ardently appeal for a mutation in psychoanalysis, for the emergence of a mutant psychoanalysis, one equal to the paradigm shift we are experiencing.

Perhaps this process of transformation alone, terrible and devastating as it may seem to you, now deserves the name of psychoanalysis.

Sources

Janine Chasseguet-Smirgel, *The Body as Mirror of the World*, translated by Sophie Leighton (Free Association Books, London, 2005)

Colette Chiland, "Problèmes poses aux psychoanalystes par les transsexuels" ["Problems posed by transsexuals to psychoanalysts"], *Revue Française de psychanalyse*, 2005, 2 Vol. 69, p. 563–577

Marcel Czermak et Henry Frignet Ed., *Sur l'identité sexuelle: à propos du transsexualisme* [On Sexual Identity: Concerning Transsexualism], (Association freudienne internationale, 1996)

André Green, "'Genèse et situation des états limites" ["The Origin and Status of Borderline States"], in Jacques André et al., *Les états limites. Nouveau paradigme pour la psychanalyse*, (PUF, 1999)

Helen King, *The One-Sex Body on Trial: The Classical and Early Modern Evidence* (Ashgate Publishing, 2012)

Thomas Laqueur, *Making Sex, Body and Gender from the Greeks to Freud*, (Harvard University Press, 1992)

Bruno Latour, *Chroniques d'un amateur de sciences*, "Avons-nous besoin de paradigmes?" [*Chronicles of a Science Buff*, "Do we need paradigms"] (Presses des Mines, 2006)

Catherine Millot, *Horsexe: Essay on Transsexuality*, translated by Kenneth Hylton (Autonomedia, 1990)

Michelle M. Sauer, *Gender in Medieval Culture* (Bloomsbury, 2015)

Note from the Translator

I feel it is important to explain the origins and importance of the École de la Cause Freudienne (School of the Freudian Cause). One of the central figures of twentieth-century psychoanalysis in France, Jacques Lacan, was the subject of considerable controversy among Freudian psychoanalysts worldwide. In the early 1960s, the failure of the negotiations between the Société Française de Psychanalyse (French Society for Psychoanalysis) and the International Psychoanalytical Association led to Lacan and his followers being excluded from the IPA, and the dissolution of the Société Française de Psychanalyse (French School of Psychoanalysis). Two new French organizations emerged: the Association Psychanalytique de France, which joined the International Psychoanalytical Association, and the Société Française de Psychanalyse, founded by Lacan which was later renamed the École Freudienne de Paris (Freudian School of Paris). In 1980, Lacan dissolved the EFP and launched the Cause Freudienne (Freudian Cause), but when this was met with recriminations and the departure of several key directors, Lacan established the École de la Cause Freudienne (ECF, School of the Freudian Cause) as his base.

Paul B. Preciado is the author of *An Apartment on Uranus*, *Counter-Sexual Manifesto*, *Testo Junkie: Sex, Drugs and Biopolitics* and *Pornotopia*, for which he was awarded the Sade Prize in France. He was Head of Research of the Museum of Contemporary Art of Barcelona (MACBA) and Director of the Independent Studies Program (PEI) from 2011 to 2014. From 2014 to 2017 he was the Curator of Public Programs of documenta 14. He is currently the Resident Philosopher at the Centre Pompidou and lives in Paris, France.

Frank Wynne has translated works by authors including Michel Houellebecq, Patrick Modiano, Jean-Baptiste Del Amo, Javier Cercas, Carlos Manuel Álvarez and Virginie Despentes. His work has earned various awards, including the IMPAC Dublin Literary Award and the Independent Foreign Fiction Prize; he has twice been awarded both the Scott Moncrieff Prize and the Premio Valle Inclán.